*Quick*GUIDES

everything you need to know...fast

Marketing

by Kylie Jones

reviewed by Sophie Moss

WIREMILL
PUBLISHING LTD

Across the world the organizations and institutions that fundraise to finance their work are referred to in many different ways. They are charities, non-profits or not-for-profit organizations, non-governmental organizations (NGOs), voluntary organizations, academic institutions, agencies, etc. For ease of reading, we have used the term Nonprofit Organization, Organization or NPO as an umbrella term throughout the *Quick* Guide series. We have also used the spellings and punctuation used by the author.

Published by
Wiremill Publishing Ltd.
Edenbridge, Kent TN8 5PS, UK
info@wiremillpublishing.com
www.wiremillpublishing.com
www.quickguidesonline.com

British Library Cataloguing in Publication Data
A catalogue record for this book is available from the British Library.

ISBN Number 1-905053-20-7

Printed by Rhythm Consolidated Berhad, Malaysia
Cover Design by Jennie de Lima and Edward Way
Design by Colin Woodman Design

CONTENTS

MARKETING

Introduction

So, What is Marketing?

Market Research and Analysis

Know How to SWOT

Setting Goals and Objectives

Developing a Workable Plan

Meeting Supporter Expectations

Is it Working?

The Ethics of Marketing

Concluding Comments

INTRODUCTION

Today, there are many organisations chasing the same 'charity dollar'. Why a person chooses to support your organisation over another one can have a lot to do with your marketing program and how successfully you promote your cause. Marketing is an important component in the operations of any business, particularly nonprofits, and everyone in your organisation - from the receptionist to the board of directors - has a role to play.

This Quick*Guide* to Marketing aims to clearly outline the basic principles of marketing and how you can apply them to your own nonprofit organisation. It is intended to act as the 'kick start' to understanding marketing and applying this knowledge to formulating a successful marketing program for your organisation.

From this Guide, you will learn the basics of:
- market analysis: what you need to know about your organisation, your supporters and other organisations working in your field (your competitors)
- how to set strategic marketing goals and objectives for your organisation
- how to develop a workable marketing plan
- the importance of after-marketing in meeting supporter expectations and building loyalty; and
- how to evaluate the results of your marketing program.

Any time you communicate with the public it is marketing. Advertising, writing to supporters, sending out invitations to an event, public relations – all and more constitute marketing. With the principles set out in this Guide your communications will be part of a focused plan aimed toward achievable goals and beneficial to your organisation.

So, What is Marketing?

Marketing is the art of making someone want something you have.

Marketing is the action or business of promoting and selling products and services.

Marketing is the process of planning and executing the conception, pricing, promotion and distribution of ideas, goods and services to create exchanges that satisfy individual and organisational goals.

Whatever definition of marketing you use, the fundamental principle of marketing is that it encompasses everything you have to do in order to come up with a needed product and/or service, making potential supporters both aware of it and approving of it and then want to support it.

When most people think of marketing, they think mainly in terms of <u>tactics</u>, partly because tactics are the most visible aspect of marketing – for example; press and television advertising or sending out direct mail letters to supporters.

While tactics are an important part of marketing, tactics alone will not get you very far without a sound understanding of your own organisation and what you have on offer, your supporters and what they want, and other organisations and what they are doing in the area in which you work. It is this information that then helps you formulate clear marketing goals and objectives in line with your organisation's mission, and leads to the development of a marketing strategy and action plan.

Continues on next page

So, What is Marketing?

**The Four Stages of
Developing a Marketing Program**

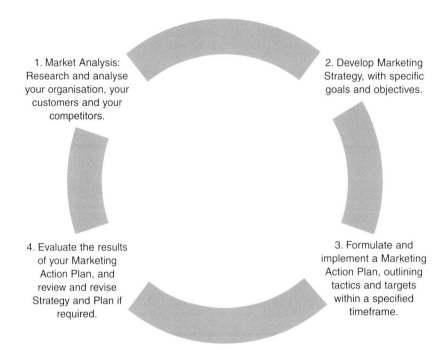

1. Market Analysis: Research and analyse your organisation, your customers and your competitors.

2. Develop Marketing Strategy, with specific goals and objectives.

4. Evaluate the results of your Marketing Action Plan, and review and revise Strategy and Plan if required.

3. Formulate and implement a Marketing Action Plan, outlining tactics and targets within a specified timeframe.

The diagram above identifies where tactics fit in the overall development of a marketing program. Before you implement marketing tactics, make sure you have taken the time to research and analyse your organisation, your supporters and other organisations, and identified clear and specific marketing goals and objectives linked to your organisation's overall mission, vision and objectives.

Know your organisation. Know your constituency. Know the other organisations in your field.

Know your organisation

To market your organisation and its work, you must first have a thorough understanding of what it does including an internal analysis of its mission and vision, organisation objectives and programs. It is also valuable to have a good understanding of the culture of the organisation and its financial and program performance to date. This information should be readily obtainable from your organisation's annual reports, website, internal documents and external publications and materials.

A useful research tool is to distribute a confidential employee questionnaire that asks peoples' opinions about the organisation, its performance and culture and to also hold interviews or discussion groups with key staff. Receiving input from many people within the organisation provides invaluable insights and also helps staff to understand and support the marketing efforts.

Know your supporters

Your market research needs to include learning as much as possible about your existing supporters and others - who they are, how they found your organisation, what they like and dislike about your organisation. It is important to remember that knowing your existing supporters can lead you to identifying potential new supporters.

A useful way to start your research is to segment everyone related to your organisation in order to help you to understand their needs and differences, and this segmentation ultimately leads to better marketing.

Groups may include:
- Donors
- Members
- Clients and/or beneficiaries
- Volunteers
- Board members
- Staff
- And any other groups who have a relationship to your programs and/or services.

Surveys and questionnaires are a way to gather useful information and to find out more about your constituent

Continues on next page

groups. There are general characteristics – or demographic information – such as age, income, gender; profession and education level; organisation or industry type; geographic location etc. and there is psychographic information that covers the likes and dislikes, opinions about the organisation and its programs, needs and desires.

When compiling a survey, it is important to keep in mind:

- The purpose of the survey – don't try and make the survey cover too many things; be specific about what you want it to achieve.

- The length of the survey – keep it fairly short, as response rates drop significantly if it takes more than 10 to 15 minutes to complete.

- The size of the sample – are you sending it to your entire list or a sample in which you need to ensure that it is random and contains enough people to be representative.

- Confidentiality – the survey must be confidential so that people will tell the truth.

- Evaluation and feedback – ensure that the survey is appropriately evaluated and discussed within the organisation, and that there are action points and/or areas of improvement prioritized for the organisation. And remember to give feedback to those involved in the survey on what the organisation has learnt and is working on as a result of the survey.

Another method of gathering information is Focus Groups. Focus Groups bring people together and ask their opinion about the organisation and its activities, and are usually conducted by a professional independent facilitator. Focus Groups take more time and effort than surveys, but the interaction of the group can lead to clearer and more in-depth information.

Telemarketing a sample of your supporters is also an effective way to gather information. This can be achieved in-house by calling people yourself and asking them to participate in a quick survey, or you can outsource to a telemarketing agency – what you do depends on what type of information you require and how many people you need to call to get that information.

Reviewer's Comment
Telemarketing is an area where you need to be very careful about what is acceptable in your country as some places it is seen as more acceptable than others.

Know other organisations
To market your organisation you need to know about other organisations. It means gathering information on their missions and visions, objectives, programs and capabilities.

Sources of information include:

- Annual reports, tax returns and other statutory requirements.

- Websites produced by the organisation.

- Opinions of your own staff, supporters and users of your services.

- Newspaper and magazine archives (many have online archive services available) for related articles;

- Private research companies regularly compile and publish data which you can obtain for a fee, and may have data collected on your competitors.

- Your local fundraising association may have a library of reference materials and also know of market research companies that may be able to assist.

- Your local library may have information on nonprofit organisations and a collection of annual reports.

- Many governmental bodies publish useful data as well as fund research on the sector.

- Some countries have 'charity commissions' or similar bodies that maintain information on nonprofit organisations that is available to the public.

In addition, a great way to keep up-to-date with a competitor's activities is to become a supporter/donor and receive regular information on its fundraising activities and services.

O ne of the most useful tools in understanding your organisation and its position within the sector is the SWOT analysis (which stands for Strengths, Weaknesses, Opportunities and Threats).

Completing a SWOT analysis helps you to identify ways to minimize the effect of weaknesses in your organisation while maximizing your strengths; and it also matches your strengths against opportunities that result from your competitors' weaknesses or possible 'gaps' in the provision of services in your area. It is important to note that the SWOT is based only on information known by you and your team, and is viewed as a more basic approach to analysing your organisation. But it is still a powerful tool when looking for immediate results and helping to formulate your marketing program.

■ Strengths allow you to focus on your organisation's Opportunities.

■ Weaknesses in your organisation can lead to Threats.

Strengths: What does your organisation do well? What makes you stand out from the competition? What advantages do you have over other organisations? What do your supporters like about your organisation? What do your employees like about the organisation?

Weaknesses: What does your organisation struggle with? What do supporters complain about? What do employees complain about?

Opportunities: Are there emerging trends externally that fit with your organisation's strengths? Try to identify and explore areas where your strengths are not being fully utilized.

Threats: Are there external threats to your organisation's success? And internally, are there financial, development or other problems that could threaten the organisation?

A Basic SWOT table is a four cell grid or four lists, one for each SWOT component. Using this table will help you organize your thoughts and information you have gathered.

SWOT Table

Internal Elements	External Forces
Strengths	Opportunities
Weaknesses	Threats

The important thing to remember is to not leave anything out – no matter how small or trivial the issue may be. And take into account that a threat can be an opportunity, and a strength can be viewed as a weakness, depending on the perspective. Be objective and at the end you should be in a position to set clear marketing objectives and to develop a marketing strategy to improve your organisation's performance.

Know the PEST Test

When you have looked at your own organisation, your supporters and your competitors, and undertaken a SWOT analysis, it is good to look at these aspects in the context of the broader environment. The easiest way is a PEST Analysis – which refers to Political, Economic, Social and Technological. Create a four cell grid, like your SWOT, and jot down the PEST factors that may impact upon or relate to your organisation and its operations.

Political	Economic
Social	Technological

Setting Goals and Objectives

Working Out What You Want to Achieve

Your marketing goals and objectives together set out **what** you are trying to achieve – do you want an increase in new supporters or to convert existing supporters into monthly committed givers; do you want to launch a new program or service and attract corporate sponsors, or increase awareness for your organisation? It is crucial that you know what your goals and objectives are before you embark on a marketing program to achieve them.

What's the difference between a goal and an objective?

A Goal is a general statement of direction – a goal often does not have measurements and specific details. An Objective is a goal that is quantified – an objective is tangible with measurable results or outcomes from your efforts.

Example:
Your overall goal may be to increase the number of new supporters to your organisation. Your objective would be to recruit and maintain a database of 25,000 new supporters in a 12 month period.

Whatever your marketing goals and objectives are, the important thing to remember is that they must be consistent with the organisation's overall mission and objectives. You need to have a clear understanding of your organisation's vision and where it is heading in order to set relevant and achievable marketing objectives.

Your marketing program will have greater success if your goals and objectives are matched to programs and services. It is important to talk with your staff and find out what the priority areas are for the next one, three or five years (depending on your organisation's planning processes).

To be able to set well-developed objectives, they need to meet the SMART criteria:

S - Specific: the objective should state exactly what is to be achieved.

M - Measurable: the objective should be capable of measurement, so it is possible to determine whether (or how far) it has been achieved.

A - Achievable: the objective should be realistic given the circumstances in which it is set and the resources available (it should also be aligned with your overall vision and organisation direction).

R - Relevant: the objective should be relevant to the people who are responsible for achieving it.

T - Time-bound: the objective should have a timeframe with a specified and realistic due date.

It is important to make sure that your marketing objectives are consistent and not in conflict with each other, and that the components of your marketing plan (such as your marketing strategy, action plan, budget, and controls and measures) support your objectives.

The advantage of setting well-defined marketing objectives and linking those to a detailed marketing strategy and plan is that it serves as a reality check for your marketing activities: i.e. do you have the resources (staffing and financial) necessary to accomplish your objectives?

The table (below) can be a handy tool for setting out your marketing goals and objectives – it may be that you have different areas of responsibility within your marketing department, and this table can help staff to bring consistency to setting objectives and to highlight potential areas for conflict (the flip side is that it can also highlight areas for potential integration of activities that could achieve greater success for your marketing efforts).

Table: Marketing Goals and Objectives

Area of Responsibility:	
Overall Goal:	(insert goal here)
Key result areas:	Objectives
1.	
2.	
3.	
4.	
5.	
6.	

Working out how you're going to achieve your objectives

Now you know what you want to achieve from your marketing, but how are you going to get there? You now need a well-constructed and realistic plan of action.

As already shown, planning involves setting objectives (quantifying targets for achievement, and communicating and agreeing to these targets with those people responsible for achieving them) and it also involves selecting strategies and tactics (strategies are **methods** chosen to achieve the objectives and tactics are the **resources** that are used).

Once you have set your marketing objectives, you then go about developing marketing strategies, and these are the medium to long-term plans that will achieve your objectives. Strategies emphasize those areas that you feel are most important to your organisation.

Generally speaking, your marketing strategies involve a mix of what is commonly referred to as the 4Ps of marketing: Product, Price, Place and Promotion.

Product – Work out the unique 'selling' point (USP) of your activities, i.e. what is worthwhile about your organisation.

Price – Price in the context of nonprofit organisations relates to donations - how much will you ask for from various types of donors, how will you support the amount of your requests, how will you encourage levels of donations and so forth.

Place – How do supporters and potential supporters find you?

Promotion – What methods do you use to tell supporters and potential supporters about your organisation? This involves advertising, public relations, direct marketing, events, word of mouth etc.

Look at the 4Ps when you are deciding on your strategies. The table (opposite) can help to consolidate your objectives, strategies and tactics for your marketing plan.

The purpose of your marketing plan is for it to act as a resource that you refer to on a regular basis that directs your activities on a daily, monthly, yearly

DEVELOPING A WORKABLE PLAN

Table: Developing an action plan from your marketing objectives and strategies

Objective:	(insert objective here)			
Strategy:	(insert strategy here)			
Tactics and Milestones				
	What to Do	By Who	By When	Completed
1.				
2.				
3.				

basis. Don't go to the effort of writing a great plan and then filing it away until next year's planning.

Don't just plan, experiment!
Effective marketing is normally developed through a combination of planning and experimentation, not just the planning alone. You will make mistakes but as long as you recognize the mistakes and learn useful lessons from them, then you can adjust the plan and try again!

Be flexible and plan for change
Flexibility is a friend of your marketing plan because things do – and will – change so your marketing plan must be able to adapt to changes. Make sure you have some contingency plans in place as this will provide you with the confidence to respond quickly to any changes that present themselves. What are the best and worst case scenarios?

Make your plan available to everyone
Ensure that your plan is user-friendly and available to all members of staff. If staff have access to it and feel they can make a contribution, you will find that they will become advocates for your marketing program.

LOYALTY: SHOWING FIRM AND CONSTANT SUPPORT; A STRONG FEELING OF ALLEGIANCE.

You've completed your marketing plan, you're getting the message out there and people are responding. You breathe a sigh of relief – your job is done! Not quite – it's just the beginning!

It's true that you need to get the supporters first; but once they're involved, you need to devote a great deal of time and energy to keeping them involved; and more importantly, you need to have a specific plan for building supporter loyalty.

Meeting supporter expectations and building supporter loyalty is an integral part of your overall marketing program and deserves as much attention as the strategies and tactics you employ. It's a well known fact that it costs far more to **recruit** a new supporter than to **maintain** an existing one; yet many nonprofits tend to concentrate their efforts on the 'front end' of marketing and fail to deliver on the 'back end'; i.e. delivering good supporter service and building loyalty.

Is Your Organisation Supporter-Focused?

The first thing to remember when devising a supporter service and loyalty plan is that it needs to involve the whole organisation. Is your organisation supporter-focused? If your staff are on side and have their own sense of loyalty to the organisation and its objectives, then it will be easier to implement strong supporter service and build loyalty with those supporters. Organisations that have earned high levels of staff loyalty have also seen high levels of supporter loyalty. Because, put simply, people 'buy into' relationships and a sense of familiarity – i.e. they want to interact with people who know them – and it's impossible to build up a rapport with supporters if there is constant turnover of staff. Invest in your staff first, so they can, in turn, serve your supporters well.

- Invite staff to be involved in planning and quality improvements for your marketing efforts.

- Use their input and involve them in decision-making.

- Implement an ongoing training process which need not be formal, but can be built around skills that have been identified by staff and are critical to your organisation's success.

- Treat staff as important partners, and they will treat supporters in the same way.

Not all supporters are equal: 80 per cent of your income is from 20 per cent of your supporters!

In nonprofit organisations, the 80/20 rule is alive and well and consequently, not all supporters are created equal. There are some supporters that represent greater long-term value than other supporters, and this is where segmentation based on value (or on RFV – Recency, Frequency and Value) comes into play. Savvy marketers will segment and monitor activities based on value to ensure that higher-value supporters receive more personalized one-on-one service with the organisation.

Establish loyalty stages and ensure that your supporters are moving through them.

This is where the supporter (or donor) pyramid is useful in order to identify your supporter segments in line with your loyalty stages. Supporters become loyal to an organisation over time and normally (but not always) one step at a time. If you understand the supporter's current loyalty stage, you can better determine what's required in relation to their supporter needs and work out ways to move them to the next loyalty stage. And if you find that

your supporters aren't moving up the pyramid, then you may need to rethink your supporter service processes.

Personalisation Scale

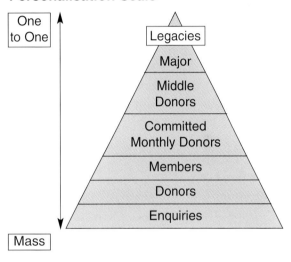

Be Responsive and Reliable

Supporters will have a sense of urgency surrounding their donation to your organisation, so it is important to share this with them - provide acknowledgment promptly and be consistent in your service. Supporter confidence in your reliability will increase your credibility and foster repeat donations. You need to assure your supporters that they will receive the same high quality service every time they have dealings with your organisation.

Continues on next page

To Meet Supporters' Needs, Know Their Needs

Demonstrate that you care about your supporters by asking them what they want – you can do this through supporter surveys or questionnaires, but also through more informal processes such as feedback forms in acknowledgment letters, online contact points or suggestion forms or simply by asking them a few simple questions the next time they call your office.

Don't ignore supporter complaints, as it's a rule of thumb that normally only 10 per cent of complaints get expressed by supporters to the organisation (but disgruntled supporters will express their concerns outside the organisation). So complaints need to be taken seriously. Establish complaint resolution guidelines which include response times and reporting procedures. Track complaint trends. Ensure that complaint calls are given the same attention as donation calls because a properly handled complaint may turn into a new donation if the matter can be resolved promptly and to the supporter's satisfaction.

Three Little Things

Most supporters of nonprofit organisations want three little things. First and foremost, they want a thank you. Secondly, they want to know where their donation is going and how it's being spent. And finally, they want to be recognized as an important part of the organisation and as such, provided with an opportunity to have a say. If you are able to meet these three needs, then you're on the right path to building supporter loyalty.

Handy Hints to Building Supporter Loyalty:

- Thank you notes
- Regular postcards
- Email updates
- Face to face information updates and supporter events
- Feedback form
- Birthday message (e.g. phone, email, SMS (text) messages, mail)
- Involvement in focus groups
- 'Special' internal communications, such as program update reports or press releases

Is It Working?

Evaluation should not be an afterthought but should form the final critical step in your marketing program. It is equally as important as setting clear marketing objectives and creating a strong marketing plan. How will you know your marketing is working if you don't take the time to analyse the results?

The purpose of evaluation is to validate what you have accomplished, and this requires both honest and objective analysis of the key areas of your marketing program, including:

- the programs and/or services;
- the supporter target groups; and
- the tactics employed in your marketing program.

Evaluation enables you to identify those areas in which a change is required, and your marketing analysis is meaningless unless it indicates some alterations that are needed to make your program better and more effective. It's worth remembering that everything can be improved upon, and it is just as important to identify the failures as it is to report on the successes!

Regular monitoring and evaluation means you will have the advantage of being able to create stronger, more effective marketing strategies over time that are more likely to achieve success, and in turn, those successes will build up credibility as a savvy marketer when you can show positive results for your organisation.

Evaluation helps you to:

- Spot weaknesses or problems that need to be addressed.
- Anticipate and take advantage of opportunities.
- Identify and amend conflicting or unrealistic goals.
- Keep on top of organisational and marketplace changes.
- Spend your marketing dollars and utilize staff more effectively.

Key things to consider when evaluating your marketing program are:

- Identify what criteria you need to be able to evaluate your marketing activity in terms of both quantitative and qualitative data.

Continues on next page

Is It Working?

- Identify the supporter group(s) that were targeted for your marketing activity, and check the response rates of supporters that responded to the marketing activity; i.e. value, frequency, any patterns and trends etc.

- Compile measurable quantitative data such as profit and loss statement, income and expenditure, return on investment, response rates, cost per response etc.

- Contact supporters for more focused qualitative feedback on a particular marketing activity, if necessary.

- Involve staff by asking for feedback on marketing activities to help evaluate the effectiveness of your marketing activities.

- Evaluate the current status of an activity against the agreed objective, timing, costs, staffing etc.

- Compare current marketing activities against previous similar activities to highlight performance and track trends.

- Summarise your evaluations and note the key points you have learned: were objectives met; what were the strengths and weaknesses; what were the results (financial and non-financial); what tactics worked and what did not; what were the areas of improvement; what are the recommendations for future activities?

- Communicate your evaluations to staff and the organisation.

Evaluation not only helps you to improve your marketing activities in the future, but it also assists to demonstrate the effectiveness of your marketing program to the Board of Directors, funders and key stakeholders in the organisation.

THE ETHICS OF MARKETING

In these days of increased accountability and public scrutiny of organisations' activities, its pays to be able to articulate a strong foundation of reasons for pursuing a particular course of action for your nonprofit organisation.

Marketing is certainly an area that is scrutinized, and from time to time, your actions may be called into question from a variety of people, including your supervisors, Board of Directors, your staff, and external stakeholders, supporters or the media.

As a marketer, you need to be aware of ethical standards and acceptable behaviour, and this awareness ought to take into account the viewpoints of four key players:

- the organisation
- the industry
- society, and
- yourself!

Ethical conflicts arise when there is a difference between the needs of the four players mentioned above; e.g. there may be a conflict of interest between what your organisation is doing in relation to the industry as a whole; or your own personal values may conflict with the activities of your organisation.

In your marketing role, you will no doubt be faced with ethical dilemmas and you will need to make a decision about the course of action to take. It can be helpful to use 'The Ethics Checklist' when making such a decision.

The Ethics Checklist involves three basic questions:

1. Is it legal?

2. Is it balanced?

3. How will it make me feel about myself?

The first question focuses on the existing standards of society, the industry and your organisation. Would your decision violate law or organisation policy?

The second question relates to your sense of 'fair play' and rationality: Would your decision be fair or does it strongly favour one party over another in the short or long term? Would your decision promote a win-win relationship?

Continues on next page

THE ETHICS OF MARKETING

The third question appeals to your own personal set of standards and emotions: how would you feel if your decision was open to public scrutiny such as published in a newspaper, or if your family and friends were told?

There are other questions that you can consider in your decision-making:

- What are the relevant facts?

- What assumptions am I making?

- What are the weaknesses in my own position?

- What will this do to my character or the character of my organisation?

- What would happen if everybody took this course of action?

- Have I considered that the means may not justify the ends?

Of course, asking these questions does not mean that you'll come up with an answer that everyone will agree on. Chances are that others will see it from a different point of view and come up with different answers.

But what is important is that the course of action is considered in terms of ethical standards and that you and your organisation embrace the opportunity to go through a process that all can agree to be thoroughly honest and competent.

CONCLUDING COMMENTS

You should now have a basic understanding of the steps involved in the process and can start to formulate your own marketing program for your organisation.

Above all, remember that marketing is a work in progress – be prepared to continually review, revise and update your marketing objectives, strategies and plans in order to reflect your results, any new information that comes to hand, and the changes that occur in your organisation and in the marketplace.

And enjoy the journey!

AUTHOR

KYLIE JONES

Kylie Jones is an Australian marketing and fundraising specialist with more than 13 years experience in the not-for-profit sector. She has had a varied career that began with postings to Somalia and Bosnia-Herzegovina to coordinate media relations for an international aid agency through to establishing and operating marketing offices in Australia and New Zealand for one of the world's largest animal protection agencies. Kylie was then posted to London to manage the agency's UK Appeals program and work in consultation with an advertising agency on a five year marketing & communications strategy.

Kylie has broad experience in the areas of marketing, fundraising, public relations, media liaison and communications. She has also been involved in field projects in countries including Borneo, India, East Timor and Indonesia.

Kylie currently runs her own consultancy business, Boomerang Marketing, from the Sunshine Coast of Queensland, Australia, and undertakes a diverse range of projects for clients including the development of fundraising and marketing strategies, website strategy and re-development, consumer education and awareness pitch campaigns, conference and event management, writing of direct mail appeals, funding submissions and publications, and media liaison.

Kylie has a Bachelor of Arts degree in Communication (major in Advertising and Marketing) and is currently studying freelance journalism.

email kj_boomerang@bigpond.com

Sophie Moss, Reviewer

Sophie Moss is a Senior Company Fundraising Executive in the Company Fundraising team at NCH, a children's charity in the United Kingdom and currently manages charity partnerships with companies including Virgin Megastores and GM Daewoo. Her experience in this field includes staff fundraising, organising national and international fundraising events and winning and establishing a variety of charity of the year partnerships.

She previously worked in Marketing for 5 years, most recently as Marketing Manager for The Leadership Trust, a provider of leadership development programmes to Directors and Senior Managers and also in export marketing in the air conditioning sector.

Sophie holds the Chartered Institute of Marketing Advanced Certificate in Marketing and a BA Hons in Russian with French and Contract Law.